THE
FUNDAMENTAL
TRUTHS

OF THE
BIBLE DOCTRINE

VOL.1

PASTOR EMMANUEL O. OLOYE

ISBN:
979 8334 232 853

Published by
PASTOR EMMANUEL O. OLOYE
Christ Miracle Church Mission,
3610 Milford Mill, Unit T3, off Liberty Road,
Windsor Mill, MD 21244,
United States.
+14436130473
Email: manueloloye47@yahoo.com
oloyeemmanuel12@gmail.com

DEDICATION

I dedicate this book to the Almighty God for His great grace upon my life and ministry.

ACKNOWLEDGEMENT

Many thanks to my father-in-the-Lord, Prophet Peter Abiola Adebisi and the entire Christ Miracle Church Mission family for their love and faithful commitment to the success of the call of God upon my life.

I want to thank my dear wife, Pastor Mrs. Modupe Oloye and our beautiful and lovely children for their patience, understanding and support of the work of God in my hand.

I acknowledge immensely Brother Adebayo Abimbola for typesetting, editing and making the production of this book a dream come true.

God bless you all.

CONTENTS

INTRODUCTION

As Christians, are intruders and sojourners in this world, where we expect the arrival of my Messiah and Christ at any moment for our ascension as pilgrims, the same way our citizenship is in heaven the expected destination of our glory. We need the knowledge of God for our guidance. Habakkuk said **"For the earth shall be filled with the knowledge of the glory of the Lord, as the waters cover the sea"** (Habakkuk 2:14), we need to tap into this in order to fulfill our purposes.

The place of knowledge cannot be underestimated as ignorance kills (Hosea 4:6), but life is replete with ocean of knowledge. Man learns to accomplish his desires, but divine knowledge enables us to accomplish God's desire. Acquiring sound education is good, but without a divine knowledge, it would not profit much. The Bible is the divine information where the believer acquires divine knowledge.

This book **"The Fundamental Truths of the Bible Doctrines"** will be of great help to all Bible students, the Believer and everyone in Christendom. There is no greater need in our

1

different Christian denominations today than for the members to be acquainted with the fundamental facts and doctrine of the Christian faith. This volume is a basis for Christianity and church dogma. The layman who desires a deeper knowledge of the doctrines of the Christian faith may find all the help needed in this book. It is a source for students learning and readable for an uninformed reader also, it is not difficult for the average layperson.

The intention of this book is to dig out the basic doctrine needed to sustain our Christian faith in this life and to eternity in the kingdom of God. Therefore, this book should be studied along side with a study Bible. It is for this reason that many of the scriptural references are indicated by chapters and verses only. There must be constant reference to the scriptures while studying.

The doctrines here are presented by the author as a systematic study from the biblical truth, compressed in topics with clear statements. The "**Outline form**" of the Bible doctrines of the evangelistic theology is also presented as an initiative of revival in a man's soul for the standard of God in conduct.

The Christian faith all over the world is being strengthened for the worldwide end time revival. The Bible promises a revival in our days, a revival of fundamental truths of the word of God. Of course, with the existence of the Social media and other

Information Technology Apps, there shall not be a scarcity of the word in our time. The word is to revive, remold, rebuild and restructure lives for the purpose of God. Therefore, our love for the truth is hereby enkindled or rekindled by the Holy Ghost as we study to know the truth.

Eschatological events (doctrine of the last things i.e. end times), were revealed to understand the futuristic event of the Bible prophecy which is yet to be fulfilled. The idea of God and salvation depravity of man and redemption, the practice of Christian doctrines and many more were revealed for our enlightenment, revival of souls and spiritual upliftment in the Christian faith.

My payer is that this book will inspire you and your appetite to read will be wet as you spend time reading and studying it. It shall be profitable to your daily spiritual upliftment and revival in the Christian faith, for the readiness of eternal kingdom in Heaven, Amen!

DIVINE INSPIRATION OF THE BIBLE

The Bible is the written word of God, the special revelation of God that comes to us in and through the bible. The Bible is God's inspired revelation to mankind, the revelation of His mind and will. God wrote part of the Bible books Himself (Exodus 31:18 32:16) God spoke some of the Bible (Matthew 3:16-17, John12:28), God dictated some of it, and moved His servants to declare the remaining parts, (Revelation 1:17-20).

It can be rightly said that the God of truth inspired some Holy men who wrote the Holy Scripture. It was written by about 40 men from different works of life. These men were moved by the Holy Ghost. The word "**Bible**" was the translation of the Greek word "**Biblos**" meaning inspired book. The Bible is not just a book, but the book that has superiority over other books. It is the basis and prerequisite for all Christian preaching and teaching. It could be described as the material form of divine revelation. Many facts prove the divine inspiration of the Bible among which are its superiority to other books; its versatility; its preservation from century to century until date, its fulfilled prophecies, perfection and power (2Timothy 3:16-17, 2Peter 1:21, Psalm 19:7-10, Isaiah 34:16, Mark 13:31). The word "Inspiration" refers to the way God's self-revelation has come to be expressed in the words of the Bible. It refers to the activities of the Holy Spirit whereby, He superintended the human authors of the scriptures so that their writing became a transcript of God's word to man. By saying that the Bible is inspired, is another way of saying that it is God's authoritative self-revelation.

The tripartite spirit of trinity was breathed through the entire Bible. God, the Father is the Source of the Bible; God, the son is the central theme of the Bible; while God, the Holy Spirit is the Author. It thus indicates that God was directly involved in the writing of the Bible.

The Bible consists of 39 books of the Old Testament and 27 books of the New Testament. We are safe and secured to rely on the Bible which is the word of God and commit our lives unto it. The word of God is given to man to save him and to keep him safe (Psalm 19:7-10, Jude 3, 1Timothy 4:16, Romans 16:17). History has it that the Bible was written over a period of 1,500 years ago. This started from the time of Moses (1,440 B.C), to the days of the Apostle John (90 A.D). Concerning the Bible and its subject materials, it takes us from eternity past, before creations (John 1:1), to eternity future, (Revelation 22:5).

THE PURPOSE OF THE BIBLE

1. To give total revelation of God to mankind.
2. To explain the eternal purpose of God.
3. To show the power and the consequences of sin.
4. To show the source, means and process of redemption of mankind.
5. To produce faith in the life of the users.

THE CLAIMS OF THE SCRIPTURES TO DIVINE INSPIRATION

The writers of the scriptures claimed to have written under the influence of the Spirit of God and there can be no doubt of this claim. The quality or degree of their inspirations may be questioned, but surely, it is not the fact of their spiritual influence.

Let us view some of the testimony of the writers:

(a)   The claims of the Old Testament writers to divine inspiration of the Bible, (Exodus 4:10-15, Deuteronomy 4:2, Jeremiah 1:7-9, Ezekiel 3:4, Micah 3:8).

These are the few of the many passages in which the inspiration of the writers is affirmed and claimed. Note further that the words **"God said"** occurred ten times in the first chapter of Genesis. It is claimed that such expression as **"The Lord said" "The Lord Spake" "The word of the Lord came"** were found 3,808 times in the Old Testament. These writers claiming their messages with the words "**Thus saith the Lord**" proved that they were not deceived in their claims, it was clear in details as to names, times, and places which characterized their messages, and from the literal fulfillment of these oracles of God.

(a)   The claims of the New Testament writers to divine inspiration of the Bible:

It was clearly noted that divine inspiration claimed by New Testament writers for Old Testament wrote as well as for themselves, (2Peter 1:20-21, 1Peter 1:10,11, Acts 1:16, Acts 28:25, 1Corinthians 2:13, 1Corinthians 14:37, 1Thessalonians 2:13, 2Peter 3:1-2, Matthew 10:20, Mark 13:11, Luke 12:12, 21:14-15, Acts 2:4).

It was evident from those and many other passages of the scripture that the writers of both the Old and New Testament were conscious of having received revelations from God, and considered themselves inspired of God to write the scriptures. They felt while writing, that they were given expression to the infallible truth of God, and were conscious that the Holy Ghost was moving them to work.

THE NECESSITY OF STUDYING THE BIBLE

It is not strange that many Christians accepted the Bible as the word of God and placed their eternal destiny upon its message. However, many fail to study its pages or heed to its precepts. All true Christians believe that the Bible is the complete and final revelation of God to man. Since God has spoken, it hardly needs to be argued that necessity is laid upon to find out what He has said.

1.   God has commanded the study of His word. The Old and New Testament alike made it clear that God never intended His people to neglect the revelation He has given. Even a king in Israel must **"Read therein all the days of his life, that he may learn how to fear the Lord His God, to keep all the words of this law and these statues, to do them"** (Deuteronomy 17:19). All of Israel was instructed to keep God's commandment in their heart to teach them diligently unto their children, to talk of them through the day, and to write them upon the post of their houses, (Deuteronomy 6:6-9). The command to God's people is **"Seek ye out the book of the law, and read, no one of these shall fail"** (Isaiah 34:16).

The New Testament is just as explicit. Christ exhorts us to **"Search the scripture, for they are they which testify of Me"** (John 5:39). The command is **"Study to show that thyself approved to God, a workman that needeth not to be**

ashamed, rightly dividing the word of truth" (2Timothy 2:15). The command has never been cancelled, it is therefore, the expressions of the present will of God. Is it not evident that a Christian who does not study God's word will stand ashamed some day in His presence, (1John2:28).

2.   The Bible is essential for **ALL AREAS OF A HUMAN'S LIFE**. It is the book to live by; it is the only book to die by. Other books inform us but the Bible alone transforms us. We must read it to be wise, believe it to be safe and practice it to be holy. We cannot know such a Book without diligence in its study. In the words of Harrick Johnson, "**If God is a reality, and your soul is a reality and you are an immoral being, what are you doing with your Bible shut**"?

In brief, the Bible is essential for salvation, (Romans 10:17), for Christian growth, (1Peter 2:2), for fellowship with Christ, (John 5:39), for purity of life, (Psalm 119:9, 11), and for effective service, (Isaiah 55:11). It is the foundation for all proper Christian living.

3.   Anti-biblical teachings must be opposed. There is so much religious dogma in the world today, contrary to the testimony of God's word. False teachings are invading our churches, our Christian literatures, and our Christian supported schools. Only God's people taught in the Bible will be able to

discern that which is of God, and that which is of Satan, (1Timothy 4:1, 2Peter 2:1-2).

For example, the documentary hypothesis (often called the J.E.D.P analysis), of German higher criticism, though exploded, but it is still being taught with gospel authority. **NEO-ORTHODOX**, a revolt with liberalism backs toward a more conservative theology, that is immensely popular, still affirms the documentary hypothesis and rejects the full inspiration of the Bible. The theory of organic evolution, now appearing in diversified form, is basically atheistic and substitutes for the motion of men for the sure word of God. Dangerous religious cults are also on the increase, introducing strange and often pagan concept under a thin veneer of Christian profession. How much we need a great host of men and women today who are dedicated to Christ and intimately acquainted with His word, to combat these errors and lead confused sinners to the Saviour.

4.   High caliber Christian leadership must be provided. The work of the Lord demands more than the half-trained and the mediocre churches, Christian schools, and other agencies are calling for leadership which is not only fundamentally sounds, but also spiritual alert, emotionally matured, and academically qualified. Today's youth will never become the spiritual leaders of tomorrow without the depth of dedication, both to the living word and the written word of God.

One of the prerequisites for studying of the Bible is proper personal attitude. Archbishop Trent once said **"The holy scripture is not a book for the slothful. It is a field, rather upon the surface of which sometimes we gather manna easily and without labor, given as it were freely to our hands, yet of which many portions are to be cultivated with pains and toils are they yield for the service of man"**.

A keen interest and a spirit of determination should characterize the believer who undertakes to study the word, to approach the Bible with a will and determination to know its message. The word of God deserves and demands our quality time and effort. **"And whatsoever ye do, do it heartedly, as to the Lord, and not unto men"** (Colossians 3:23).

Bible Study should be commenced in the spirit of prayer, asking God for needed wisdom and understanding, (James 1:5). **"Open thou mine eyes, that I may behold wondrous things out of thy law"** (Psalm 119:18).

Essential also is the earnest dependence upon the Holy Spirit, for He is our best Teacher, (1John 2:27), who guides the believer into all truths (John 16:13), and unfolding even the **"Deep things of God"** (1Corinthians 2:10, John 16:7-15 and 1Corinthians 2:9-16), are the two most important passages on the teaching ministry of the Holy Spirit. His part is to illuminate our hearts with the word and to open our to understanding it while our own part is that of daily earnest study.

THE ATTACK OF THE BIBLE

The Holy Scriptures is the collection of various writings, which the earliest part of this collection was penned by Moses; and the last by a disciple of Jesus Christ.

Efforts to silence the scriptures have a long history coming from the Common Era, through the Middle Age, down to the modern times. An early record of such effort dated back to the time of Prophet Jeremiah, a notable Prophet of God, who lived over 600 years before the birth of Jesus Christ.

Prophet Jeremiah was directed by the Lord to write a message on a scroll to condemn the sinful acts of the inhabitant of the ancient Judah and to warn them about the consequences on their capital city, Jerusalem, and how it would be destroyed except they change their ways and turn to the Lord. Jeremiah's secretary, Baruch, read the message aloud in the public in the temple in Jerusalem. He read it a second time in the hearing of Judah's princes, who took the scroll to King Jehoiakim. As the king listened to God's word, he did not like what he heard and therefore destroyed the scroll and cut it into pieces and burned it, (Jeremiah 36:1-23).

God then commanded Jeremiah "**Take thee again another scroll, and write in it all the former words that were in the first scroll, which Jehoiakim the king of Judah hath burned**"

(Jeremiah 36:28). Some 17 years later, exactly as God's Word through Jeremiah had foretold, Jerusalem was destroyed. Many of its rulers were slain, and its inhabitants were taken into exile in Babylon. The messages the scroll conveyed and a record of the circumstances surrounding the attack made upon it have survived until our days in the book of Jeremiah.

Jehoiakim was not the only person in the pre-Christian Era who attempted to burn God's word. Following the breakup of the Greek Empire, Israel came under the influence of the Seleucid dynasty. The Seleucid king, Antiochus Epiphanes who ruled from 175 to 164 BC wanted to unite his empire in Hellenistic culture. To that end, he attempted to force the Greek ways, customs and religion upon the Jews.

About 168 B.C, Antiochus robbed God's temple in Jerusalem. He plundered everything and atop the altar, he built another altar in honour of the Greek god Zeus. Antiochus also stopped the observance of the Sabbath and ordered the Jews to leave their sons uncircumcised and the penalty for their noncompliance was death.

The reason for the emergence of that religious idea was Antiochus' attempt to eliminate all scrolls of the law of the Lord. Although, Antiochus pursued his religious campaign throughout Israel, he failed to destroy all copies of the Hebrew

Scriptures. Some carefully concealed scrolls may as well, have escaped the flames in Israel and copies of the Holy Scripture were known to be preserved by Colonies of Jews living elsewhere.

Another prominent ruler who tried to destroy the scripture was the Roman Emperor Diocletian. In 303 AD, Diocletian carried out a series of increasing harsh orders pronounced by his authority against Christians. This resulted in what some eminent historians have termed "**The great persecution**" His first order was the burning of the copies of the Holy Scriptures and the demolition of Christian meeting places. Harry Y. Gamble, the professor of religious studies at the University of Virginia wrote "**Diocletian took it for granted that every Christian community, wherever it might be, had a collection of books and knew that those books were essential to its viability**". Eusebius of Caesarea, Palestine, a notable church historian who lived during the period says "**We saw with our very eyes the houses of prayer cast down to their foundation from top to bottom, and the inspired and sacred scriptures committed to the flames in the midst of the market places.**"

After Diocletian's order, the mayor of the North African city of Citra, which is now known as Constantine, is said to have ordered the Christians, to hand over all their "**Writings of the law**" and "**Copies of the scriptures**".

14

The account of the same period tells of Christians who preferred to be tortured and killed rather than hand over copies of the Bible to be destroyed.

THE INTENTION OF THE ATTACKS

The Bible survived all and every attempts to destroy it, however, the attacks on the Bible continued. As the time passed, efforts to make translation of the Bible into other languages were made as only a few could read the Bible in the Hebrew or Greek languages in which it was written. Most of us would have difficulty in understanding God's word if until today it was only available in ancient form of the Hebrew or Greek languages. Almost 300 years before the advent of Jesus Christ, efforts to translate the Bible from the Hebrews language into Greek began. The translation is known as the Greek Septuagint. Some 700 years later, Jerome produced a famous translation known as the Vulgate. This was the rendering of the Hebrew and Greek scriptures into Latin, which was the common language of the Roman Empire of that time. After some times, Latin began to fade as a common language as only the well-educated of the society maintained familiarity with it, and the Catholic Church resisted every effort to translate the Bible into other languages. Religious leader argued that Hebrew, Greek and Latin were the ones suitable for Bible languages.

The ruler and church leaders claimed that the Bible burnings were not attempts to destroy the Bible. Rather, these men were simply trying to keep the Bible out of the hand of the common people.

In the ninth century A.D, Methodius and Cyril, Thessalonian missionaries acting on behalf of the Eastern Churches in Byzantium prompted the use of Slavic as a church language. Their goal was to enable the Slavic people of Eastern Europe, who understand neither Greek nor Latin, to learn about God in their own language. These missionaries, however, met with fierce opposition from the German priests, who sought to impose Latin as a defense against the expanding influence of Byzantine Christianity. Clearly, politics was more important to them than the people's religious education. Increasing tension between the Western and Eastern branches of Christendom led to the division between the Roman Catholicism and Eastern Orthodoxy in 1054.

Roman Catholicism eventually came to view Latin as a holy Language. Thus, in response to the request made in 1079 by Vratislatus, the Duke of Bohemia, eventually sought the permission of the Slavonic in local church services to do so. Pope Gregory VII wrote: **"We cannot in any way grant this petition"** and why not? **"It is evident that those who consider the matter carefully"**. **That it has pleased God to make the**

Holy Scripture obscure in certain place lest, if it were perfectly clear to all, it might be vulgarized and subjected to disrespect or be so misunderstood by people of limited intelligence as to lead them to error." The common people were given limited access to the Bible in several manners, and it had to stay that way. This stand afforded the clergy the power over the masses. They did not want the common people to dabble into the areas they considered to be their own domain.

In 1199, Pope Innocent III, wrote concerning **"heretics"** who had translated the Bible into French and dared to discuss it among themselves. To them Pope, Innocent applied Jesus' statement **"Give not that which is holy unto the dogs, neither cast ye your pearls before swine, lest they trample them under their feet, and turn again and rend you"** (Matthew 7:6), what was his reason in this matter? **"That no simple and unlearned men presume to concern himself with the sublimity of the sacred scripture or to preach it to others"**. Those who resisted the Pope's order were often delivered to inquisitor's who had them tortured into making confessions. Those who refused to withdraw or recant were burned alive.

During the long battle fought over the possession of the Bible and the reading of it, Pope Innocent's letter was often appealed to for support in forbidding the use of the Bible and its translation into other languages. Sometime after his decree, the burning of the Bibles in the vernacular began, as did the burning of some of their owners. In the centuries that followed, the Bishops and rulers of the Catholic in Europe, used all possible means to ensure that the ban imposed by Pope Innocent III was observed.

The Catholic hierarchy certainly knew that many of its teachings were solely not based on the Bible but also on Church tradition and the Magisterium. This was one of the reasons for their reluctance to allow their faithful access to the Bible. By the priests and church hierarchy alone reading the Bible, the people would become aware of the incapability between the Church doctrine and the scriptures.

EFFECT OF THE REFORMATION ERA ON THE BIBLE ATTACK

The arrival of Protestantism took over the space from the then church leaders and brought luke-warmness and spiritual lethargy to the Christian faith and this transformed the Europe's Christianity landscape. We have many reformers during the Era of Martin Luther's attempt to reform the Catholic Church and his eventual break in 1521, as this was based essentially on his understanding of the Scriptures. So, when that break was complete, Martin Luther, a gifted translator, endeavored to make the Bible available to the public.

Martin Luther's translation into the German language and its wide distribution got the intension of the Roman Catholic Church. Which felt that Luther's Bible ought to be offset by the one accepted by the Church. Two such translations in the German language soon appeared. But in 1546, less than 25 years after the Roman Catholic Church of Trent, in an effort, placed the printing of religious literature including translations of the Bible, under the control of the Church.

The council of Trent decreed **"That henceforth, the sacred Scriptures be printed in most correct manner possible, and that it shall not be lawful for anyone to print, or cause to be printed, any books whatever on sacred matters without the name of the author or in future to sell then, or even to possess them, unless they shall have been first examined and approved of by the local Bishop"**.

In 1559, Pope Paul IV, published the first index of books rejected by the Roman Catholic church. It forbade the possession of the Bible translations in Dutch, English, French, German, Italian and Spanish, as well as some in Latin. Anyone who wanted to read the Bible was told to obtain written permission from Bishops or inquisitors and not from an appealing prospect, for those who wanted to remain above suspicion of heresy.

The people who dared to possess or distribute the Bible in the common languages of their regions, had to contend with the fire of the Catholic Church. Many were arrested, burned at the stake, roasted on spits, sentenced to life imprisonment, or sent to galleys and the confiscated Bibles were burned. Indeed, the Catholic priests continued to confiscate and burn Bibles well into the 20th century.

This is not also saying that the Protestantism has been a real friend and defender of the Bible. In the 18th and 19th Centuries, some protestant theologians with their championed techniques of study came to be known as higher criticism. In time, many people accepted the teachings as influenced by Darwinian theories that life was not created but somehow appeared by chance and evolve without a creator.

Theologians and even many clergymen taught that the Bible is largely based on the legends and myths. As a result, it is common today to hear the protestant clergymen, as well as many of their parishioners, disclaim the Bible, saying it is unhistorical.

Perhaps you have noted the critical attitude of the Bible's authenticity and maybe you are surprised at the attempts that were made to destroy it in the past centuries and those attacks however, all failed. The Bible survived them all.

WHY THE BIBLE SURVIVED THE ATTACKS

Honestly, many have loved the Bible and have been willing to lay down their lives to defend it. The key to its survival however, lies in a Divine influence greater than human love. The simple reason for the survival of the Bible is that all writers of the Bible wrote them under the divine inspiration of God.

Reading and applying what the Bible teaches improve the human life in all ramifications, both spiritually and physically in term of moral conduct. By these, we know more about God and serve Him endlessly to enjoy His eternal blessings thereafter. Therefore, God desires the Bible to survive all the attacks and to be translated into many languages for the benefits of all and sundry in humanity.

The Bible is God's means of providing answers to the questions of the Christian faith, (John 17:17). The Bible which is the word of God is the carrier of His power and Christians who believe to deal with the enemies and the challenges of life and also to survive the issues of life will always find it a vital tool.

The divine inspiration of God's message found in the Bible through the writers is the only hope of the believer in life and eternity.

②
TRINITY
OF THE GODHEAD

The Godhead consists of three separate, distinct and recognizable personalities with different qualities perfectly united into one. The Father, the Son and the Holy Ghost are different persons in the Godhead, but not merely names for one person rather for three distinct persons. Great is the mystery of the Trinity. There is one God, who is the Father of our Lord Jesus Christ. The loving God and Father gave His only begotten Son, Jesus Christ to the world, in order for us not to perish, but have everlasting life for the Father loveth the Son, and hath given all things into his hand, (John 3:16, 35). The given Son is also the mighty God and the everlasting Father, (Isaiah 9:6). The Son spoke of the Father in (John 4:23-24), as being Spirit in (Acts 5:3-4), and the Holy Spirit is called God. How wonderfully and perfectly blended together then is the Trinity? The Trinity of the Godhead is co-existing, co-eternal, and co-equal in power and divine attributes. To deny the Trinity is to deny God. However, it is wonderful to know the Trinity and enjoy their ministries in your life, 1Corinthians 12:4-6, (Matthew 28:19, Matthew 3:16-17, Luke 3:21-22, John 10:30).

THE TRINITY OF THE GODHEAD IN THE OLD TESTAMENT

The Hebrew has the plural, singular forms and dual using of the word, for the expression of God. These classifications are seen below:

Elohin: This is the Plural word that signifies a number that is more one or two.

Elohahim: This is a dual word that signify a number that is more than one but not more than two

Elohi: This is a singular word that signifies a number that is not more than one.

There are three monotheistic religions in the world: Judaism, Christianity and Muhammadaism. The second is a development of the first while the third is an outgrowth of both. But Judaism accused Christianity of Polytheism for the reason of believing in the Trinity as it believes in monotheism. Christians are not worshiping many gods but one God in three persons, Elohim.

The unity is essential to the Godhead as three in one. The issue of the Trinity is incomprehensive to the natural human knowledge, but scripturally believable to the spiritual understanding.

a.   The Father is not God as such, for God is not only the Father, but also the Son and the Holy Spirit.

b.   The son is not God as Such, for God is not only the Son but also the Father and the Holy Spirit.

c.   The Holy Spirit is not God as such, for God is not only the Holy Spirit, but also the Father and Son.

The burden of the Old Testament message seems to be on the unity of God, as the word "**Trinity**" was not mentioned anywhere, yet the doctrine of the Trinity is clearly embedded in a four-fold way.

1.   In the plural name of the deity for example, Elohim, etc.

2.   The personal plurals use for our God, is often used in plural pronouns in speaking of Himself, for example, (Genesis 1:26) "Let **us** make man" (Isaiah 6:8) "Who will go for **us**" (Genesis 3:22) "Behold, man is become as one of **us**".

Some would say that the "**us**" in (Genesis 1:26) "let **us** make man" refers to God's consultation with angels with whom He takes counsel before He does anything of importance; but in (Isaiah 40:14), the Bible says "But of whom **He** takes Counsel" shows that such is not the case; and (Genesis 1:27), contradicts the idea, for it repeats the statement "In the image of God" not in the image of angels.

3. The Theophanies, especially the angel of the Lord, (Genesis 16:18), this shows that God reveals Himself in Angelic manner in the Old Testament.

4. The work of the Holy Spirit, (Genesis 1:2, Judges 6:34), God revealed Himself in form of the Spirit.

THE TRINITY OF THE GODHEAD IN THE NEW TESTAMENT

The doctrine of the Trinity is clearly taught in the New Testament; it was not merely intended, like in the Old Testament, but explicitly declared as the evidential proof.

1. The Baptismal of Christ in Matthew 3:16-17. Here, the Father spoke from heaven as the Son is being baptized at the Jordan and the Spirit descended in the form of a dove.

2. In the Baptismal Formula, (Matthew 28:19) "**Baptizing them in the name of the Father, and of the Son, and of the Holy Ghost**".

3. The Apostolic Benediction; 2Corinthians 13:14 "**The grace of our Lord Jesus Christ, the Love of God and Communion of the Holy Ghost**".

4. Christ Himself teaches in (John 14:16) "**I will pray the Father and He will give you another Comforter**".

5. The New Testament sets forth:

The Father is God, Romans 1:7

The Son who is God, Hebrew 1:7

The Holy Spirit who is God, Acts 5:34.

THE TOTAL DEPRAVITY OF HUMAN RACE

Sinfulness and the guilt of man since the fall of Adam, rendered man a subject to God's wrath and condemnation, (Job 14:4, Romans 15:12-17, Mark 7:21-23, Ephesians 2:1). By the term **"Total Depravity"** we refer to the inheritance of sinful nature by man, through the voluntary disobedience, transgression and fall of man into the depth of sin. The natural man is a bond-slave to sin. His sinful nature is the outcome of the terrible fall of man in the Garden of Eden. Man is naturally inclined to evil and his entire nature, mentally, morally physically and spiritually is affected by sin.

Only God can save a sinful man, and deliver him from his sins, (Romans 3:9, 23, Psalm 51: 5, 58:3, Genesis 6:5-7, Isaiah 53:6). Have you been totally delivered from depravity? An entire change of heart called regeneration is the remedy for human depravity, (2Corinthians 5:17). The Bible teaches that the heart of man is deceitful, above all things and desperately wicked. None can know his heart. No man totally knows his heart, if the heart which is the best in man is desperately evil and wicked beyond knowledge, how terrible must the total man be?.

THE NATURE OF SIN

Through the Bible, it is believed that sin is the cause of the total depravity of the human race. There are varieties of terms used in the Bible to describe the nature of sin which include:

❖ It is the expression of the thought of missing the mark, (Exodus 32:30).

❖ It is the expression of the thought of rebellious acts and trespass or transgression of the God's will, (Proverbs 28:13).

❖ It is the expression of going astray, (Leviticus 4:13).

❖ It is the expression of the thought of failure, fault and concrete wrong, (Matthew1:21).

❖ It is the ideas of unrighteousness or injustice, (1Corinthians 6:8).

❖ It is the ideas that refers to the breach of law, (Romans 4:15).

❖ It is the expression of the thought of lawlessness.

❖ It is the reflection of the strong sense of godlessness, (Titus 2:12).

The effects of sin, in relation to God;

a. It makes us unfit for God's presence and brings spiritual separation. We cannot enjoy the intimacy of His presence when we have sin in us, (Genesis 3:23).

b. It hinders us from doing God's will. Our will has lost its freedom to sin's comfort against the divine purpose of God and became enslaved to sin, (Romans 7:21).

We are unrighteous before God's law. Therefore, we are subject to the curse of the law, (Deuteronomy 27:26, 28, Romans 3:19, 5:16, Galatians 3:10).

d.   We are insensitive to God's word. Sin brings us to a state of ignorance of God and unable to understand the things of the Spirit.

In relation to our neighbours, sin:

a.   It brings conflict

b.   It causes exploitation as we make our neighbours scape-goats for our own frustrations and sense of guilt. We use them rather than loving them. Our giving is a means of getting.

c.   Fear: We try to hide our identities

d.   Misunderstanding: This also continues even when there is a genuine desire to know and to be known.

In relation to oneself, it causes:

a.   Inner conflict, (Romans 7:23).

b.   Self-Deception, (1 Corinthians 4:3).

c.   Shame, (Genesis 3:7-8),

d.   Restlessness, (Isaiah 57:20),

Finally, in relation to time:

a.   Our days are numbered

b.   It leads to anxiety

Undoubtedly, sin has affected us and broke the relationship between us and God. Man was total depraved and in need of redemption which only God can give.

4

REDEMPTION
OF THE HUMAN RACE

Redemption is God's way of buying back the human race that was sold to sin and the dominion of satan through the disobedience and fall of man in Eden. "Redemption" is the wonderful story of God's act through Christ to bring the lost man back to Himself. "Redemption" is the wonderful story of how Jesus paid the price of our release from captivity and death, in order to be made free unto God, (Romans 5:12-17, Isaiah 53:3-6, 1Corinthians 6:19-20, Matthew 26:28).

Redemption is allied with salvation, but it is more specific, although a means of salvation. Salvation may bequeath temporary and physical deliverance; but redemption has to do with the re-buying of properties. In the ancient Israel, both persons and property could be redeemed. The deliverance of Israelites from Egypt is spoken of as redemption. Man is seen as an object of redemption and God as the Redeemer. Christ is seen in the New Testament as the Redeemer, (Luke 2:38, 24:21, Galatians 3:13, 4:5). This expression was metaphorically used in Galatians that redemption was spoken of as "The deliverance of the Christian Jews from the Law of Moses and its curse".

Paul also spoke of "**Redeeming the time**" or buying up the opportunity in (Ephesians 5:16 and Colossians 4:5). By the usage of redemption in this context, Paul was telling the saints to make the most of every opportunity by turning each opportunity to the best advantages since none can be recalled if missed.

In Redemption, there is need for ransom to be paid. This is what Christ did. He was the Lamb that was slain, from the foundation of the world (Revelation 13:8). When we look at what the Scriptures say about man's condition, we will be quick to learn that at the fall of Adam, man became a slave to sin, the flesh, and the devil. Therefore, in order to deliver mankind from this slavery, Christ paid the ransomed price and bought man out of such slavery condition with the intention of setting the purchased slave free.

Romans 6:16-17, speaks of the slavery that every son of Adam inherited. The word "**Servant**" in these verses literally means slave. The picture the word of God is presenting by the use of this word is that, any slave being purchased out of the slave market of sin by Christ, such purchased possession now belongs to Christ who would demand obedient service from His newly-purchased slave. But Christ will not force any creature to serve Him. Even though He owns the redeemed individual; He sets that redeemed individual free.

The redeemed is no longer obligated to serve sin (as his master), but free to choose who he will serve. The ideal response to this newly freed slave of sin is to freely choose to be the slave of Christ who delivered him from the cruel master he had served.

In the sixth Chapter of the book of Romans, we see that man was destined to always be a slave to someone or something. But experience has shown that man will either serve sin or he will serve righteousness, for Christ is the Christian's righteousness.

It is completely a lie of the devil to tell man that he can do anything he wants and that man is not obligated to serve anyone but him. We need honesty to acknowledge that no man is completely free to do whatever he wants. There are a number of forces controlling man, demanding him to do or act in ways contrary to his personal choice, government, society, family and God's law, all these make their demands upon mankind and the individual is not free to do as he pleases. Since every man will serve one form of master or the other, why not serve the Creator God who has the only authority in heaven and on earth, who always wants the best for His servants?

To see that the redeemed individual does not own himself, 1Corinthians 6:19-20, say "Know ye not that your body is the temple of the Holy Ghost which is in you, which ye have of God, and ye are not your own?.

? For ye are bought with a price: therefore glorify God in your body, and in your spirit, which are God's".

It is now obvious that redemption from the curse of the law, healing of sicknesses and diseases as well as good health are provided for all people through the sacrificial death of Jesus Christ, (Exodus 15:26, Deuteronomy 7:15, Psalm 103:1-5, Proverbs 4:20-22, Isaiah 53:4,5, Matthew 3:16,17, 1Peter 2:24, Mark 16:15-18, Luke 13:16, John 14:12-14, 10:10, Acts 10:38, James 5:14-16, 1John 3:8, 3John 2, Galatians 3:13-14).

REPENTANCE JUSTIFICATION AND NEW BIRTH

epentance is the change of the penitent mind and attitude towards sin, which makes a man to turn from his sin to God. It is a deep inward experience and change, (2Corinthians 7:10, Luke 5:8). 2Corinthians 7:11, x-rayed the seven attitudes in repentance which comes as a result of godly sorrow for sin.

1. It works carefulness in the penitent.
2. It makes the penitent seek to cleanse himself from his guilt by restitution.
3. It produces indignation towards sin and the occasion of sin.
4. It results in the fear of God and to dread sin.
5. It produces the desire to please God for the rest of one's life.
6. It spurs zeal for God and for righteousness in the penitent.
7. It turns him against Satan and the flesh for revenge.

The word repentance has two basic meaning in the Hebrew concept:

a. **Naham** - This word refers to a man's repentance or repenting. It literally means pant or groan.

b. **Shub** - This means to turn or return. This has to do with a change of mind with godly sorrow for what one has done wrongly. It is to feel humiliated for what you have done that could be seen as unheard of in the society. This is not applicable to God, (Numbers 23:9, Genesis 6:5-7). Therefore, the basis of repentance does not lie on "**Naham**" but on "**Shubh**" which is to turn back and away from the wrong and towards, the right, especially in the religious sense.

Repentance has three aspects that help to lead to a change of heart. They are: Intellectual, Emotional and Volitional.

INTELLECTUAL ASPECT: This is the recognition of one's sinfulness and helplessness. It is the awareness of one's sinful condition and a personal knowledge of sin, (Romans 3:20, Romans 7:7).

EMOTIONAL ASPECT: This consists of a feeling of godly sorrow for sin and a sense of humiliation, (2Corinthians 7:9,10). It is the aspect knowledge that leads to the acceptance of Christ.

VOLITIONAL ASPECT: This is the change of purpose. It is the inward turning from sin to Christ, (Acts 2:37-42). The nature of repentance is not self-punishment, or making oneself as an atonement or self-reformation. It is a change of heart, (Luke 15:11-21), to forsake one's old way of sin.

Therefore, repentance is the complete turning away from all sins and its deceitful pleasures that is required of every sinner before he can truly and effectively believe in Jesus with saving faith, (Proverbs 28:13, Isaiah 55:7, Ezekiel 18:21, Mark 1:15, Luke 24:46,47, Acts 2:38, 3:19, 20:20-21, 2Corinthians 7:10, Hebrews 6:1-3).

JUSTIFICATION

By justification, we mean the act by which the penitent sinner is granted pardon on the basis of Christ's atonement for him, (Romans 5:1-10). The greatest need any individual must have is to be made righteous. This is because only the believers, who are righteous according to God standard, will be able to stand in His presence. This is because every son of Adam inherited sin and there is no way any man can attain to this righteousness by self-efforts. With this understanding, God devised a plan whereby men who have been found guilty can be given Christ's righteousness (2Corinthians 5:21). This process is called "**Justification**". Justification is when God imputes Christ's righteousness to the guilty.

This imputation of righteousness comes when we accept Christ's as our Lord and Saviour. In (Romans 4:25), Paul says that righteousness was imputed to anyone who would **"Believe on Him who raised up Jesus our Lord from the dead who was delivered for our offenses"**.

In the quoted text, we see that Christ was **"Delivered for our offenses"** and He died for debt of our sins. If we will only trust Him who raised up Christ and believe that all we need to do is to appreciate His forgiveness through faith and by acknowledging that the blood of Christ which was shed when He died, was because of our sins, then, God will give us Christ righteousness as a free gift. This truth is as recorded in (Romans 4:25), for Paul said that Christ **"Was raised for our justification"**. It was necessary that Christ be raised, in order for us to be justified. That is, for us to be made righteous, (2Corinthians 5:21).

NEW BIRTH

New birth is the process by which God recreates the sinful man to become righteous, (John 3:3-7, 2Corinthians 5:17).The scripture makes it clear that the sinner is outside the family of God, and as such has no right to a home in heaven. Through the miracle of the new birth, the one who believes in Christ receives a spiritual rebirth and life which will in turn position him in the family of God. He is **"Regenerated"** (Titus 3:5), and becomes a **"Born again"** child of God, (1Peter 1:23).

It is said that George Whitfield preached over three hundred times on the text **"Ye must be born again"** (John 3:7). When he was asked the reason, he solemnly answered **"Because ye must be born again"**. The new birth is divinely imperative. Anyone without Christ is dead to sin, (Ephesians 2:1-3), self-improvement will not avail, nor is self-help possible, (Ephesians 2:8-9). The only cure for spiritual DEATH is spiritual BIRTH, and it can only be bestowed as a gift from above to the regenerated soul. The Bible says **"The wages of sin is death, but the gift of God is eternal life through Jesus Christ our Lord"** (Romans 6:23, 1John 5:12).

The Bible uses many approaches to clarify its presentation of the way of NEW BIRTH, although, the illustration and the terminology may differ greatly. But there remains throughout eternity one central truth of the forgiveness of sin through a new relationship to the son of God. As we deal with sinners concerning the new birth experience and their spiritual need, we should **"Vary our approach"** and use the illustration which will be the more helpful. These then, are not different ways to be saved, for Christ alone is the way of the new birth experience. These are merely different illustrations of what it means to receive Christ, but could be presented differently depending on the situation, so that all may understand and in faith come to Him.

SOME IMPORTANT BLESSINGS THAT ACCOMPANY NEW BIRTH

• WE HAVE THE FORGIVENESS OF SIN:
Forgiveness of sin is available to the believer by the virtue of the substitutionary death of Christ on the cross, (1Peter 3:8, Ephesians 1:7). It has been said that Mohammed, upon his death bed, ordered the execution of his enemies. But in contrast, the prayer of Christ on the cross is for His Father to forgive His executioners "**Father forgive them for they know not what they do**" (Luke 23:24, John 1:29, Colossians 1:14).

• WE ARE IDENTIFIED WITH CHRIST:
In His death, burial and resurrection, (Romans 6:4-5, Colossians 3:1-3), Christ identified Himself with our sins and paid its penalty to the full, (Isaiah 53:5-6). When believers identify themselves with Christ, the Father identifies us in the finished work of Calvary. Not only are we viewed as crucified with Christ, (Galatians 2:20) and rose to the newness of life (Romans 6:4), but also seated together in the heavenly places (Ephesians 2:6). The new birth of those who are in Christ is certain as in their faith, they are being observed by the Father as already in heaven.

• WE RECEIVED THE GIFT OF RIGHTEOUSNESS:

It is only God that removes the penalty of sin from the regenerated soul. He bestows upon us the gift of righteousness on a basis that the sinner may stand before Him as acceptable, (Romans 3:22, 5:17, 2 Corinthians 5:21, Philippians 3:9). When the process of new birth is taking place in the life of a sinner, he will be clothed with a garment of the righteousness of Jesus Christ. How is CLOTHING used to picture the spiritual condition? A sinner dare not stand before the Holy God in a filthy garment or unrighteousness, (Isaiah 64:6). Rather, he would be clothed with the white linen of Christ righteousness, (Revelation 3:4-5, 19:8,14). Isaiah 61:10, says "I will greatly rejoice in the Lord, my soul shall be joyful in my God; for He hath clothed me with the garments of salvation, He hath covered me with the robe of righteousness, as a bridegroom decketh himself with ornaments, and as a bride adorneth herself with her jewels". This Old Testament passage beautifully captures the garment of salvation and the robe of divine righteousness. The imputation of the righteousness of Christ to the believer is just as real as the transfer of human guilt to Christ. Not only has the record of our account cleared, we have been "**Accepted in the beloved**" (Ephesians 1:6). We will stand some day before the Righteous Judge of the universe and hear Him say "**Go, you have been forgiven**" which is better than to hear man say "**Come, for you are worthy**". It is His righteousness that is transferred to our account that makes us worthy.

• WE ARE THE CHILDREN OF GOD:
"**Beloved, now are we the sons of God**" (1John 3:2, 2Corinthians 6:18). "**The Spirit Himself beareth witness with our spirit, that we are the children of God**" (Romans 8:16). To become a member of God's family can only be accomplished through a new birth experience. The authority for this is none other than Christ Himself, who declared expressly that "**Ye must be born again**" (John 3:3,7). According to (John 3:5), this "**New Birth**" is accomplished by two AGENCIES:

a.   The word of God, here is symbolized by water that cleanses, (Ephesians 5:26, John 15:3).
b.   The Holy Spirit, (Titus 3:5, John 1:13, 1Corinthians 12:36), in the believer's heart which makes one a child of God.

We are "**Born again, not of corruptible seed, but of incorruptible, by the word of God, which liveth and abideth forever**" (1Peter 1:23).
Two great privileges are included in these miracles:
1.   Eternal life is granted as a gift from God, (Romans 6:23, John 10:28, Ephesians 2:1, 1John 5:12).
2.   The believer is received into the membership of the family of God, (Ephesians 3:15, 2:19). This family relationship establishes the basis upon which Christians can be forgiven and cleansed from the defilement of their present sins (1John 1:6, 2:2). Sonship likewise, guarantees our future glory with Christ, (1 John 3:2).

40

- **WE ARE ADOPTED OF GOD:**

Somebody who once testified "**Praise God, I am not an adopted son of God, but a real son**" gave evidence of not knowing what adoption is. It is not a substitute for sonship, but an additional privilege. In reality, the truths drawn from human family relationship are necessary to convey the fullness of our relationship with Christ. Adoption adds the thought of maturity in the realm of privilege and responsibility. While it is true that in the realm of spiritual growth and Bible knowledge, he may still be a "**Babe in Christ**" (1Peter 2:2). Nevertheless, he is not viewed as a helpless infant. Upon salvation, he has the throne, the privilege of prayer. Immediately, he has the responsibility of living and witnessing for Christ. Adoption stresses the fact that the new Christian has privilege and responsibilities which could never be accorded to an infant. For he stands before God with the stature of an adult son, (Galatians 4:5, Romans 8:15, Ephesians 1:15).

- **WE ARE HEIRS OF GOD:**

(Romans 8:17, Galatians 4:7) Heirship has to do with our spiritual inheritance to the sonship of Christ. It is the thought that we are viewed first as "**First born sons**". In many cultures, family title, lands, and goods are inherited exclusively by the first born son, lest anyone from such a background wonders what his inheritance might be in Christ. The Lord clarifies the fact that our inheritance is full and complete, as enjoyed by the first borns.

Having been given the best gift, the Father will not withhold any good thing from us. With the understanding that He lavished His love upon the Son, He will not also withheld His love from those who are "**Joint heirs**" with Him (Romans 8:32, Titus 3:7).

• WE ARE IN THE FAMILY AND HOUSEHOLD OF GOD (Ephesians 2:19):

A Believer must have relationship with other believers. We are brothers and sisters in Christ, and together we comprise a new fellowship, a spiritual household. There are responsibilities within the household of faith. We are to pray one for another, (Ephesians 1:15-16) and to help and encourage one another, (Romans 14:19). In one word, we are to love one another even as Christ has loved us and gave His life for us, (John 13:34-35, Romans 13:8,10, Hebrews 10:24-25).

• WE ARE NOT UNDER THE LAW:

How thankful we must be that the church is not under the Mosaic Law which could neither save nor bless, but only condemn, (Galatians 3:10, John 1:17, Galatians 2:16,21). Paul in particular makes it clear that we are dead to the law and delivered from its bondage, (Romans 7:4-6, Romans 8:2). Christ has fulfilled the law, taking it out of the way and nailing it to His cross, (Colossians 2:14). This is not merely the Jewish ceremonial law, but the entire Decalogue, the ten commandment

"Written and engrave in stones" (2Corinthians 3:7). Remember, the law was very harsh and stern to the people under it, (Exodus 31:12-17, 35:2-3, James 2:10). Today, Christians are not under the law, but under grace, (Romans 6:14). They are not bound either by the Mosaic Law or by the Leviticus system.

However, we are not lawless and left to walk without standards. All the issues of life are guided by the well stated New Testament commandments, which required a heavenly standard of life suitable to for heavenly-bound believers, (Philippians 3:20). But the exhortation is no longer **"I command you"** but **"I beseech you"** (Romans 12:1). The appeal is no longer fear, but the law of love, (John 14:15,21). The Mosaic Law and Leviticus order of the Old Testament were not eradicated, but they have been elevated and restated to the church of the New Testament, for the New Testament is the fulfillment of the Old. The entire book of the Galatians was written to demonstrate that the law has no binding force on the Christians, either by way of the new birth or as a role of life. **"Christ has redeemed us from the curse of the law"** (Galatians 3:13). Praise God for the liberty. However, grace gives us no license to sin, (Romans 6:1-2).

WE HAVE ACCESS TO GOD, (Ephesians 2:18): There is a prayer fellowship with God available to the believer at the moment of his conversion. As a new born child of God, you can petition Him as His Father, (Matthew 6:8-9). You may now ask and believe that your joy may be full, (John 16:24).

43

You may no longer need an earthly mediator, no priest, no potentate, but can come directly to the Father, in the name of Jesus, (1Timothy 2:5).

The saints of the Old Testament approached the presence of God with fear, but the New Testament church have free access to their Father, (Hebrews 12:18-24). The wonderful privilege of prayer that is yours as a believer must never be underestimated.

• **WE ARE PARTAKERS IN A FOURFOLD MINISTRY OF THE HOLY SPIRIT:** There are four distinct ministries of the Holy Spirit which is performed with the believer at the moment of his new birth.

a. We are "**Regenerated**" by the Holy Spirit, (John 3:1-7). It is the spirit of God who grants the believer life and positions him in the family of God.

b. We are "**Indwelt**" by the Holy Spirit (1Corinthians 3:16, 6:19-20). Every believer's soul is the temple of the Holy Spirit. He has taken up His residence within us. And the absence of the Holy Spirit indicates the lack of a new birth.

c. We are "**Baptized**" by the Holy Spirit, (1Corinthians 12:13). The ministry of the Holy Spirit joins both the Jew and the Gentile believers together as members of His church, which is the Body of Christ in this present age.

d. We are "**Sealed**" by the Spirit, (Ephesians 4:30). Every believer has been sealed unto the day of redemption.

The Spirit Himself is the evident seal, and His presence implies ownership and security on the believer.

• WE ARE IN THE KINGDOM OF GOD AND OF CHRIST:

There is a present spiritual kingdom in addition to the future, earthly reign of our Lord. (Colossians 1:13) suggests that the entrance into the sphere of God's dominion over us involves a two folds movement.

a. We are delivered from the kingdom of Satan and the power of darkness. Satan ones held us in his dreaded away because of our sin (Ephesians 2:2, 1John 3:8) and our participation in the satanic world system (1 John 5:9, Acts 26:18)

b. We are translated into the kingdom of God's son. We have been broken from Satan's control by the reason of the new birth and enlist in the army of Jesus Christ (2 Timothy 2:4, Ephesians 6:10-17).

• WE HAVE RECEIVED A NEW NATURE:

We have seen that all men have inherited a fallen nature as a direct consequence of Adam's sin. Now a believer, while still possessing the old nature, has also a new nature from God received at the new birth (2Corinthians 5:17, Ephesians 4:22-24, Colossian 3:5-10). Man's old nature has been judged by Christ on the cross (Romans 6:6) we are to reckon ourselves as dead to it (Romans 6:11) and by yielding (Romans 6:13-19) and the control of the indwelling spirit (Romans 8:1-13) enter into lasting victory over its power.

- **WE ARE ROYAL PRIESTHOOD:**

The ordination and clerical vestment is not what makes the believer Christ's priest, but the saving faith in Christ which makes him both a king and a priest unto God, (Revelation 1:6, 20:6). Peter acknowledged that believers in general constitute the "**Royal priesthood**" before God (1Peter 2:9).

What then are the duties of a priest?

Primarily, the duties of a priest are two: That of "**Sacrifice and of intercession**". As our great High priest, Christ has offered Himself as an acceptable sacrifice for the sins of men, (Hebrews 9:11-14, 10:10-14). As our priest "**He ever liveth to make intercession**" for us (Hebrews 7:25). The role of the believer as priest is to intercede for all men, (1Timothy 2:1), and to render unto God the sacrifices of praise, (Hebrews 7:25), of the earthly goods (1Corinthians 16:2), and your body a living sacrifice, (Romans 12:1). To offer unto God our worship, our stewardship, and our complete being is indeed, a reasonable service for us who are the recipient of His wonderful grace. These are some of the privileges available to every believer purchased by Christ and made available at the moment of his new birth in Christ.

46

6

WATER BAPTISM

ater Baptism is essential our obedience to be complete in Christ after being reconciled with God. Water Baptism is done by **"Immersion" "In the name of the Father, and of the Son and of the Holy Ghost as Jesus commanded"** (Matthew 28:19-20). Water Baptism is a biblical rite through which a saved soul is symbolically buried with Christ and raised up with Him, to walk in the newness of life. Christ was baptized to teach us to do likewise and to fulfill all righteousness. He commanded that all who accept the saving gospel through faith must be baptized. It is a necessary mark of the beginning of the new life and an act of obedience to the gospel, (Romans 6:3-4, Matthew 3:13-15).

Although, water baptism is administered to a saved soul yet that Bible says **"He that believeth and is baptized shall be saved"** (Mark 16:16). For a person to profess salvation and yet refuse, avoid or be unwilling to be baptized is a proof of not being saved. However, if someone is baptized by water without a deep understanding of the gospel and without true salvation experience, such baptism is not recognized in heaven. The process is after coming to the knowledge of truth, the normal .

steps must be taking, (Acts 19:1-5).

Baptism by immersion in water is one of the ordinances of the church of Christ, and was observed by Christ Himself and then, the Apostles and the early disciples, (Acts 2:38, 40-42, 8:12-13, 9:18, 10:47-48). It is clearly a symbol of the believer's identification with Jesus Christ in His death, burial and resurrection, (Romans 6:3-4). Hence, only the believer in Christ should be baptized, and soon after his conversion, (Acts 16:15, 33, 18:8, 19:5). Acts 8:36-38, makes it crystal clear that baptism should follow after salvation and not precede it.

The mode of baptism that is highly disputed is well-know. However, since baptism is a public testimony that the believer is in Christ when he was judged for sin, that he was buried with Him and has risen with Him to the newness of life, it seems fair to say that the symbol which corresponds most closely with the things symbolized is in all probability the correct one.

It is wise at this point to respect the views of others, and to recognize that certain Scriptures may visualize the baptism of the Spirit rather than water baptism, (Mark 16:16, Galatians 3:27, Ephesians 4:5). Matthew 28:19 gives certain instructions, while repentance and faith, (Acts 2:38) and (Acts 18:8), say it should precede baptism just as the newness of life should follow it, (Romans 6:4).

7

SANCTIFICATION

◆●◆

The word "**Sanctify**" and "**Holy**" can substitute each other. They both come from the same Greek word "**Hagios**" which means to set apart. What would a believer be set apart from? It is from evil, sin and Satan in order to be set apart unto God. These two thoughts are prominent in this definition "Separation from evil, sin and Satan, and dedication unto God and His services in the kingdom. This setting apart may have no moral connotation, (Leviticus 27:14,16, Exodus 13:2, Jeremiah 1:5, John 10:36), and may also have, in which case, a person is cleansed from moral defilement. This is the main focus of the meaning, as this is very necessary, (Hebrews 12:14). Sanctification is the will of God for every Christian, (1Thessalonians 4:3-4), it is also God's command for everyone, (1Peter 1:15-16).

If regeneration or new birth has to do with our nature, justification with our standing and adoption with our position, then sanctification has to do with our character and conduct. In justification, we are declared righteousness. Justification is what God does for us, while sanctification is what God does in us.

49

While justification puts us into a right relationship with God, sanctification exhibits the fruit of a life separated from a sinful world and dedicated unto God.

The target of sanctification is self. Sanctification is a definite Christian experience, subsequent to the new birth. By this experience the believer is made pure and holy in heart and consecrated and enabled to cleave to God in life and service without the slightest tendency to want to go astray or away from the Lord. Entire sanctification is indispensable for the heaven bound saint, (Philippians 1:20-21). God the Father who is the Godhead of the Trinity is the Author of sanctification; (John 17:17, 1Thessalonians 5:23, Hebrews 12:9-10). God the son (Hebrews 10:10, 13:12, Ephesians 5:25-27), and God the Holy Spirit, (Romans 15:16, 1 Peter1:2). What defiles a man is the evil that proceeds out of his heart, (Mark 7:20-23, Galatians 5:19-21, Ephesians 5:1-5, 2Timothy 3:1-5, Revelation 22: 14-15).

These seven facts are clearly distinguishes sanctification:
1.   Sanctification makes your heart right with God, (Psalm 27:8).
2.   Sanctification makes you free from easily besetting sin or involuntary transgression.
3.   Sanctification joins your heart with God in an inseparable union (Romans 8:35-39, Philippians 1:20-21).

4. Sanctification enables the believer to be freely united with other believers, without compromise and yet without hypocrisy.

5. Sanctification is the strength of the heart in moral battles in life.

6. Sanctification is the key to the Pentecostal experience of the baptism of the spirit.

7. Sanctification is the passport to heaven, (Hebrews 12:14).

CERTAIN ASPECTS OF SANCTIFICATION

1. INSTANTANEOUS AND POSITIONAL SANCTIFICATION:

This is the position of holiness where a Christian is brought into the New Birth, based on the work of Christ, (1 Corinthians 1:2,30, 6:11, Ephesians 1:1, Hebrews 10:10). By the death and resurrection of Jesus Christ the sanctification of the believer takes place at once. The very moment a man believes in Christ, he is sanctified, that is, in this first stage, he is separated from sin and separated unto God and for this reason, all through the New Testament, believers are called saints. If a man is not a saint he is not a Christian; if he is a Christian he is a saint. Some Christian doctrines believe people are canonized after they are dead; the New Testament canonizes believers when they are alive. In (1 Corinthians 6:11), **"Sanctified"** is put before **"Justified"**. The believer grows in sanctification by a simple act of faith in Christ, that makes it happen once. Every Christian is a sanctified man. This same act that ushers him into the state of justification admits him once into the state of sanctification, in which he is to grow until he attains the fullness of the measure of the stature of Christ.

2.   PRACTICAL AND PROGRESSIVE SANCTIFICATION:

This is the progressive working out of your position in your practical life, (Philippians 2:12, Colossians 3:8-12). It is viewed as a process by an instantaneous act which simultaneously carries the idea of growth into completion, (2Peter 3:8, 2Corinthians 3:18). The fact that there is always danger of contracting defilement by contact with a sinful world, and there is an ever increasing sense of duty and deepening consciousness of sin in the life of genuine believer. This necessitates a continual growth and development in the grace and virtues of the believer's life. There is **"Perfect holiness"** (2Corinthians 7:1). God gave us the five-fold ministry for the perfection of the saints, (Ephesians 4:11-15).

MEANS OF PROGRESSIVE SANCTIFICATION

1.   Identification with Christ, (Romans 6:1-14).
   a. You should know that you are in Christ, free from sin and dead to sin, (Galatians 5:24).
   b. You should reckon your position in Christ into your life daily, (Galatians 5:20),
   c. You should yield your body to God.
2.   You should allow the Holy Spirit to control your life, (Ephesians 5:18, Galatians 5:16).
3.   You should give yourself to the word of God, (Psalm 119:11, John 17:17).

4.   You should not play with sin rather call it its real name and avoid places of temptation.

5.   You should accept chastisement from God, (Hebrews 12:10-11, John 5:16-17).

COMPLETE AND FINAL SANCTIFICATION:

This is the consummation of our sanctification at the coming of our Lord, when we shall be removed from the presence of sin and Satan (1Thessalonians 3:13, 1John 3:2). The Bible also says "And the very God of peace sanctify you **wholly,** and I pray God your whole spirit and soul and body be preserved blameless unto the coming of our Lord Jesus Christ" (1Thessalonians 5:23). "**Wholly**" means to be complete in every part and perfect in every respect whether it refers to the church as a whole, or to the individual believer. Someday, the believer would be all complete in every area of his Christian character as no Christian grace will be missing. To be complete in the "**Spirit**" links him with the heavenly, in the body links him with earth and in the soul is where the heavenly and earth play. This blessing of the entire and complete sanctification will take place when Christ comes.

8

THE HOLY
SPIRIT BAPTISM

The Holy Spirit is the third personality of the Trinity. His Baptism in a believer's life is the work of grace in our Christian faith. The Holy Spirit Baptism is an indispensible experience by which a believer is promised the endowment of power from on high. This baptism is for the purpose of a **believer's endowment of the power for service,** and the believer's edification. The believer's endowment of power for service, and the believer's edification, the believer's enlightenment in deep spiritual things and the believer's triumph in spiritual warfare, (John 14: 16-18, 26, 15:26, 16:1-13, Acts 1:4-5,8, Luke 24:48-49, Acts 2:1-4, 14-18, 19:1-7).

The ministry of the Holy Spirit in a believer's life is essential with specific intentions, purposes and assignment to be fulfilled. If the four mentioned attributes in the first paragraph are important to be believer, he will abandon all else to seek the experience. The Holy Spirit is to be yearned for and received once and for all. Therefore, nothing should hinder the flow and experience of the Holy Spirit, after you have experienced the Scriptural salvation.

The power for service and triumph in spiritual warfare is undeniable and a non-controversial evidence for receiving the Holy Spirit baptism. All believers need the baptism in the Holy Spirit, (Matthew 3:11, John 20:22, 7:37-38).

We are living in the era of the Holy Spirit, the era of grace. The Old Testament period could be called the era of the Father, for it was the period that the gospel of redemption was proclaimed. The era of the son was from the day of Pentecost until the day of His ascension after which the Holy Spirit era took over.

All matters pertaining to the doctrine of the Holy Spirit should be of special interest to the believer of this era that is so blessed with special privileges. Our churches and fellowships must beware of the ignorance on the matters of the Holy Spirit, as Apostle Paul warned in (1Corinthians 12:1). The Holy Spirit is the life behind every of Christianity even unto eternity.

THE PROOF IS THE PERSONALITY OF HOLY SPIRIT.

It is difficult to define a personality, especially when it is used for the Divine Being. God cannot be measured by any human standard for He was not made in the human image. It is man that was made in the image of God. The Holy Spirit has human personality. The name "**Comforter**" was given to Holy Spirit, which means He s the One called to your aid, as a client calls the service of a lawyer, (John 14:16,16:7). The word "**Spirit**" is a neutral agenda, although the Greek word uses it for "**Wind**" and "**Spirit**". The Authorized Version of the Bible uses neuter pronoun "**Itself**". The name "**Comforter**" cannot be used for any abstract thing, even Bible uses masculine pronoun for the Holy Spirit. These scriptures help to explain it better, (1John 2:1, Romans 3:26, John 16:7,8,13-15,1John 2:6,3:3,5,7,16). The Holy Spirit is identified with the Father and the Son and with Christians in such a way as to indicate personality, (Matthew 28:19, 2Corinthians13:14, Acts15:28).

The Holy Spirit possesses intellectual ability and capability. He has the quality and enabling power of searching the deepest and profoundest truths of God, and possessing the knowledge of God's counsel sufficiently to understand His purpose, (1Corinthians 2:10-11). A mere influence could not do this, these scriptures can attest, (Isaiah 11:2-3, 1Peter 1:11). The Holy Spirit is said to have a "**Mind**" which implies thought, purpose and determination, (Romans 8:27). The mind is an attribute of personality. He is the source of deep knowledge for all believers.

The Holy Spirit has a quality of emotion. He is very sympathetic, and the reason He is the **"Comforter"**. He feels for us and may be grieved (Ephesians 4:30). He could be insulted (Hebrews 10:29), lied against, (Acts 5:3), blasphemed and sinned against, (Matthew 12:31-32). Surely, He is susceptible to personal treatment.

The Holy Spirit possesses the quality of sensitivity. He has the ability to perceive or to be conscious of what we do. He is sensible to our attitude in our day to day Christian walk which is the reason "When He comes, He will reprove the word of sin and righteousness, and of judgment, (John 16:8-11). The Holy Spirit speaks, (Revelation 2:7, Matthew 17:5, Acts 10:20). Speech is an attribute of a personality. It is the Spirit who speaks through the apostles, (Matthew 10:10). The Spirit maketh intercession, (Romans 8:26, Hebrews 7:25, 1John 2:1, 2), where Christ is said to **"Makes intercession"** (Acts 13:2, 16:6-7, 20:28). In these Bible passages, the Holy Spirit is seen calling missionaries, overseeing the church, and commanding the life and practice of the apostle and the whole church, such acts indicate a personality.

THE PROOF OF THE DEITY OF THE HOLY SPIRIT

The deity of the Holy Spirit is meant that the Holy Spirit is God. The fact is clearly established in the Scriptures, in a five-fold way:

1.   **HIS DIVINE NAMES:** The Holy Spirit is called "**God**" in (Acts 5:4). This is opposed to man. Also in (2Corinthians 3:17-18), the Holy Spirit is called "**Lord**" for the meaning of the "**Lord**" is seen under the deity of Christ.

2.   **HIS DIVINE ATTRIBUTE:** He is eternal in nature, (Hebrews 9:14). He is Omnipresent (Psalm 139:7-10), Omnipotent (Luke 1:35) Omniscient (1Corinthians 2:10-11). The meaning of these attributes is seen under the doctrine of God and Jesus Christ.

3.   **HIS DIVINE WORKS:** The Creation, (Genesis 1:2, Psalm 104:30) "**The spirit of God hath made me, and the breath of the Almighty hath given me life**" (Job 33:4), regeneration, (John 3:5-8), resurrection, (Romans 8:11).

4.   **HIS ASSOCIATION WITH THE FATHER AND THE SON:** The Holy Spirit is on equality with the Father and the Son (Matthew 28:19, 2Corinthians 13:14, Acts 15:28), including the distribution of Spiritual gifts, (1Corinthians 12:4-6).

5.   The Bible passages which in the Old Testament refer to God are also in the New Testament referring to the Holy Spirit. Let us compare (Isaiah 6:8-10) with (Acts 28:25-27), and (Exodus 16:7) with (Hebrews 3:7-9).

THE NAMES OF THE HOLY SPIRIT

Just as the Father and the Son have various names ascribed to them, to prove their nature and works, so does the Holy Spirit have names which indicate His Characters and works.

1. **THE HOLY SPRIT,** (Luke 11:13): the Holy Spirit possesses holiness in His character, (Romans 1:4). The Spirit is holy in Himself and produces holiness in others.

2. **THE SPIRIT OF GRACE,** (Hebrews 10:29): As the executive of the Godhead, the Holy Spirit confesses the God's grace. To resist the Holy Spirit is to shut off all hope of salvation. To resist the His appeal is to insult the Godhead.

3. **THE SPIRIT OF BURNING FIRE,** (Matthew 3:11, 12, Isaiah 4:4): This cleansing is done by the explosion of the Spirit's burning. Here is the searching, illumination, refining and gross-consuming character of the Spirit. He burns up the flaws in our lives when He enters and takes possession.

4. **THE SPIRIT OF LIFE,** (Romans 8:2): The Holy Spirit is the power of the believer's experience that treads him into a life of liberty and power.

5. **THE SPIRIT OF TRUTH,** (John 14:17, 15:26, 16:13, 1John 5:6): As God is Love, so is the Holy Spirit. He possesses, reveals, confers, leads into, testifies to, and defends the truth. He opposes the "**Spirit of errors**" (1John 4:6).

6. **THE SPIRIT OF PROMISE,** (Ephesians 1:13): The Holy Spirit is the fulfillment of Christ's promise to send the comforter, and so He is the promised Spirit. The Holy Spirit also

confirms and seals a believer, and thus assures him that all the promises made to him shall be completely fulfilled.

7. **THE SPIRIT OF GLORY,** (1Peter 4:14)**:** Glory as used in the scripture means character. The Holy Spirit is the one who produces God-like character in the believer, (2Corinthians 3:18).

8. **THE SPIRIT OF GOD AND CHRIST,** (1Corinthians 3:16, Romans 8:9)**:** The fact that the Spirit is sent from the Father and the Son, means that He represents them, and being the third member of the executive, seems to be the thought conveyed here.

9. **THE SPIRIT OF WISDOM AND KNOWLEDGE,** (Isaiah 11:2, 61:1-2)**:** This is the Spirit that abides with the Messiah, it is clearly established in, (Luke 4:18). "**Where Spirit**" is capitalized. Christ's wisdom and knowledge manifest in one aspect of the case, from His being filled with the Spirit. "**Wisdom and knowledge**" refer to the intellectual and moral apprehension. "**Counsel and might**" is the power to scheme, originate and to carry out. "**Knowledge and the fear of the Lord**" is the acquainting with the true will of God, and the determination to carry it out at all cost. These graces are the results of the Spirit's operations in a life.

10. **THE COMFORTER,** (John 14:16, 16:7)**:** This indicates that the Holy Spirit comforts the heart of believer. He is the Adviser we consult, and He gives us counsel and directs our minds in the will of God. David said "**Thy rod and thy staff they comfort me**" (Psalm 23:4). The Holy Spirit comforts us with the word of God to give respite and relaxation to our souls.

THE WORK OF THE HOLY SPIRIT

The work of the Holy Spirit is universal. In relation with the world and humanity as a whole; He is in a believer's life, with reference to the scriptures and Jesus Christ.

1. THE WORK OF THE HOLY SPIRIT IS UNIVERSAL, (Psalm 33:6). This portion attributes of the work of creation to the Trinity. (Job 33:4), attributes the creation of man to the Holy Spirit. It is good to say that the Father created all things through the support of the word (His Son) and the Holy Spirit. In the Genesis account of creation, the Spirit is seen actively engaged in the work of creation, (Genesis 1:3). The power of the Holy Spirit is the preservation of the nature (Isaiah 40:7).

For humanity as whole, it is the work of the Holy Spirit to constantly bear witness of Christ and His finished work of grace to the world of sin. This He does universally, although hardly and exclusively, through the testimony of believers to the saving power and work of Christ, (John 15:26-27, Acts 5:32). The Bible established three distinct facts about the work of the Holy Spirit in (John 16:8-11). First, He will let humanity know the meaning of the sin of unbelief in Christ. This is absolutely true concerning all that Christ is and His claims to be; that the power of Satan and sin had been broken. The second is of righteousness, the Holy Spirit will enable the world to know that the righteousness in which all other righteousness will be manifested and fulfilled. The third is of judgment, the Holy Spirit will make the world to know that the judgment in which all other judgments are decided and grounded. Of sin belongs to man; of righteousness belongs to Christ, and of judgment; belongs to Satan.

1. **THE WORK OF THE HOLY SPIRIT IN A BELIEVER**

a.   He regenerates the believer, (John 3:3-5, Titus 3:5).

b.   The Holy Spirit indwells the believer, (1Corinthians 6:19, 3:16, Romans 8:9, 1 Corinthians 12:3). No matter how imperfect a believer may be or how immature his Christian experience is, he has the indwelling of the Spirit, (Acts 19:2) does not contradict.

c.   The Holy Spirit seals the believer, (Ephesians 1:13, 14, 4:30, 2Timothy 2:19-21). Believers are sealed unto the day of redemption. The seal stands for two things; ownership and likeness. The seal has to do with the heart and the conscience, satisfying both as to the settlement of the sin and sonship questions, (Galatians 4:6, Romans 8:14-16).

d.   The Holy Spirit in-fills the believer, (Acts 2:4, 4:31). There is the difference between possessing the Holy Spirit and being filled with the spirit. All believers have the first and not all have the second. Although, all may have the infilling but (Ephesians 4:30), speaks of the believers as being "**Sealed**". He commands the same believers to "**Be filled and to being filled again and again with the Spirit**" (Ephesians 5:18).

The Holy Spirit seeks for the active men who are not merely possessed but also being filled with the Spirit for service, (Acts 6:3, 5, 9:17, 11:24). Possession gives assurance, while infilling is for the service.

a.   The Holy Spirit empowers the believer for life and service (Romans 8:2, 9-11). The believer possesses the nature of flesh and the spirit, (Galatians 5:17), but the believer does not live after the flesh (Romans 8:12, 13). The Holy Spirit enables the believer to get constant and continual victory over sin, (Galatians 5:22,23), these also go against (Galatians 5:19-21).

b.   The Holy Spirit is the guide of the believer's life, (Romans 8:14, Galatians 5:16,25). The Holy Spirit guides a believer's daily life as he walks in the Spirit, under the control and direction of the Holy Spirit's Steps (Psalm 37:23).

He also guide the believer as to the field in which he should labour (Acts 8:27-29, 16:6-7, 13:2-4).

c.   The Holy Spirit anoints the believer: The anointing stands for three things;

i.   For knowledge and teaching, (1John 2:27, 2:20, 1Corinthians 2:9-14, John 14:26, 16:13).

ii.   For service, (Luke 4:18), Jesus depended on the power of the Spirit for the success of His ministry.

iii.   For consecration: There are three classes of people anointed in the Old Testament; the Prophets, the Priests, and the Kings. This was the essence of concentration. For the New Testament, the Holy Spirit anoints all who believe in Christ Jesus.

THE WORKS OF THE HOLY SPIRIT IN RELATIONS TO THE SCRIPTURES

a.   He is the author of the Scriptures. The Holy men of God Spoke as they were moved by the Holy Spirit, (2Peter 1:20,21), the Scriptures came by the inbreathing of God (2Timothy 3:16). **"Hear what the spirit saith to the churches"** (Revelation 2 and 3). It was the Holy Spirit who was to guide the apostles into the truth, and show them the things to come, (John 16:13).

b.   The Holy Spirit is also the Interpreter of the Scripture (1 Corinthians 2:9-14). He is **"The Spirit of wisdom and revelation"** (Ephesians 1:17). **"He shall receive of me and show it unto you"** (John 16:14,15).

THE WORK OF THE HOLY SPIRIT IN RELATION TO JESUS CHRIST

a.   Christ was conceived by the Holy Spirit, and born of the Spirit, (Luke 1:35).

b.   He was led by the Spirit (Matthew 4:1).

c.   He was anointed by the Holy Spirit for service, (Acts 10:38).

d.   He was crucified in the power of the Holy Spirit, (Hebrews 9:14).

e.   He was raised by the power of the Holy Spirit, (Romans 1:4, 8:11).

f.   He gave commandment to His disciples and the church through the Holy Spirit (Acts 1:2).

g.   He is the bestowal of the Holy Spirit (Acts 2:33).

OFFENCES AGAINST THE HOLY SPIRIT

Offences against the Holy Spirit can be classified under two general categories.

1. **OFFENCES COMMITTED BY THE UNBELIEVER BY:**
   - Resisting the Holy Ghost, (Acts 7:51, Acts 6:10, Acts 7:51-57).
   - Insulting or despising the Holy Spirit, (Hebrews 10:29, Luke 18:32).
   - Blaspheming the Holy Spirit, (Matthew 12:31-32).

2. **OFFENCES COMMITTED BY THE BELIEVER BY:**
   - Grieving the Holy Spirit, (Ephesians 4:30-31, Isaiah 63:10). To grieve means to make sad or sorrowful, (Galatians 5:17-19).
   - Lying to the Holy Spirit, (Acts 5:3,4), on the case of Achan, Joshua 7), on the case of Gehazi, (2Kings 5:20-27).
   - Quenching the Holy Spirit, (1Thessalonians 5:19, Matthew 12:20, Ephesians 6:16).
   - **Resisting** the word of God may have to do with the deactivation of the regenerating work of the Holy Spirit.
   - **Grieving** may have to do with annoying the indwelling Holy Spirit.
   - **Quenching** may have to do with extinguishing the inducement of the Spirit in service.

Made in the USA
Columbia, SC
03 April 2025

56084780R00039